DEAR GURTUG,
I AM THANKFUL YOU ARE IN MY CLASS THIS YEAR.
I HOPE YOU ENJOY THIS BOOK AND IT
REMINDS YOU OF OUR FIRST ART LESSON TOGETHER.
MRS. PHILIP :)

By Monica Kulling

Illustrations by Dean Griffiths

pajamapress

This is a first edition.

10 9 8 7 6 5 4 3 2 1

www.pajamapress.ca info@pajamapress.ca

The publisher gratefully acknowledges the support of the Canada Council for the Arts and the Ontario Arts Council for its publishing program. We acknowledge the financial support of the Government of Canada through the Canada Book Fund for our publishing activities.

Library and Archives Canada Cataloguing in Publication

Kulling, Monica, 1952-, author When Emily Carr met Woo / by Monica Kulling ; illustrations by Dean Griffiths.

"This story drew its inspiration from Emily Carr's The Heart of a Peacock, first published by Oxford University Press, 1953"--title page verso. ISBN 978-1-927485-40-8 (bound)

1. Carr, Emily, 1871-1945--Juvenile fiction. 2. Woo (Monkey)--Juvenile fiction. 3. Monkeys--Juvenile fiction. I. Griffiths, Dean, 1967-, illustrator II. Title.

PS8571.U54W54 2014 jC813'.54 C2013-907301-9

Publisher Cataloging-in-Publication Data (U.S.)

Kulling, Monica, 1952-

When Emily Carr met Woo / Monica Kulling ; Dean Griffiths.

[32] pages : col. ill. ; cm.

Summary: A struggling painter who bred dogs to make ends meet, Emily Carr was thought crazy for trading a puppy for a sad monkey in a pet store. Woo the monkey made plenty of mischief, even eating a tube of toxic paint, but she also brought much joy to Emily's life.

ISBN-13: 978-1- 927485-40-8

1 Carr, Emily, 1871-1945 – Juvenile fiction. 2. Woo (Monkey) – Juvenile fiction. 3. Monkeys – Juvenile fiction. I. Griffiths,Dean, 1967-. II Title.

[E] dc23 PZ7.M6543Wh 2014

Manufactured by QuaLibre Inc.
Printed in the United States of America

Pajama Press Inc.
112 Berkeley St. Toronto, Ontario Canada, M5A 2W7

Distributed in the US by Orca Book Publishers
PO Box 468 Custer, WA, 98240-0468, USA

This story drew its inspiration from Emily Carr's *The Heart of a Peacock*, first published by Oxford University Press, 1953.

IMAGES: Dust Jacket/Cover: Emily Carr, *A Skidegate Pole*, 1941-1942, oil on canvas, Collection of the Vancouver Art Gallery, Emily Carr Trust; Emily Carr, *Big Raven*, 1931, oil on canvas, Collection of the Vancouver Art Gallery, Emily Carr Trust, Photography: Trevor Mills, Vancouver Art Gallery; Emily Carr, *Lone Cedar*, Accession number 1994.056.001, courtesy of the Art Gallery of Greater Victoria; *Emily Carr with her monkey, Woo*, Image I-61505 courtesy of Royal BC Museum, BC Archives. **Page 32:** *Elephant*, Image B-09610 courtesy of Royal BC Museum, BC Archives.

The original art is rendered in watercolor and pencil crayon.

For Nancy, lover of the Emily poems
–M.K.

For my dad
–D.G.

Folks in Victoria didn't understand Emily Carr's art.
They thought the painter was a strange bird.

She lived with all sorts of animals—dogs, cats, a parrot named Jane, and a rat named Susie. She walked around town pushing a baby stroller filled with puppies.

One day, the strange bird went to the pet shop to buy birdseed. From behind a crate, a tiny face stared back at her.

Emily’s heart went out to the small creature. “Will you trade a puppy for that lonely monkey?” she asked.

The small creature perched on Emily's shoulder as she walked home. A sea breeze ruffled the monkey's fur. The air smelled of kelp and salt and faraway places.

"Woo-woo-woo!" she shrieked.
"I will call you Woo," said Emily.

Woo loved pranks. She pulled puppy tails, chased the cats, and grabbed Jane's feathers. Whenever she pulled out a plume, Woo whooped through the house.

“Woo-woo-woo!”
“Stop pestering Jane!” Emily would shout.
But teasing Jane was too much fun.

Emily's sisters Alice and Lizzie lived nearby. When they first met Woo, the little monkey whisked Alice's hat off her head and pounced on Lizzie's shoulders.

"Eeeek!" Lizzie shrieked.

The cherries looked real, but they tasted awful. Woo spat them out.
“This monkey can’t stay,” said Alice.
“This monkey has to go,” agreed Lizzie.
But the sisters could see that Woo made Emily happy.

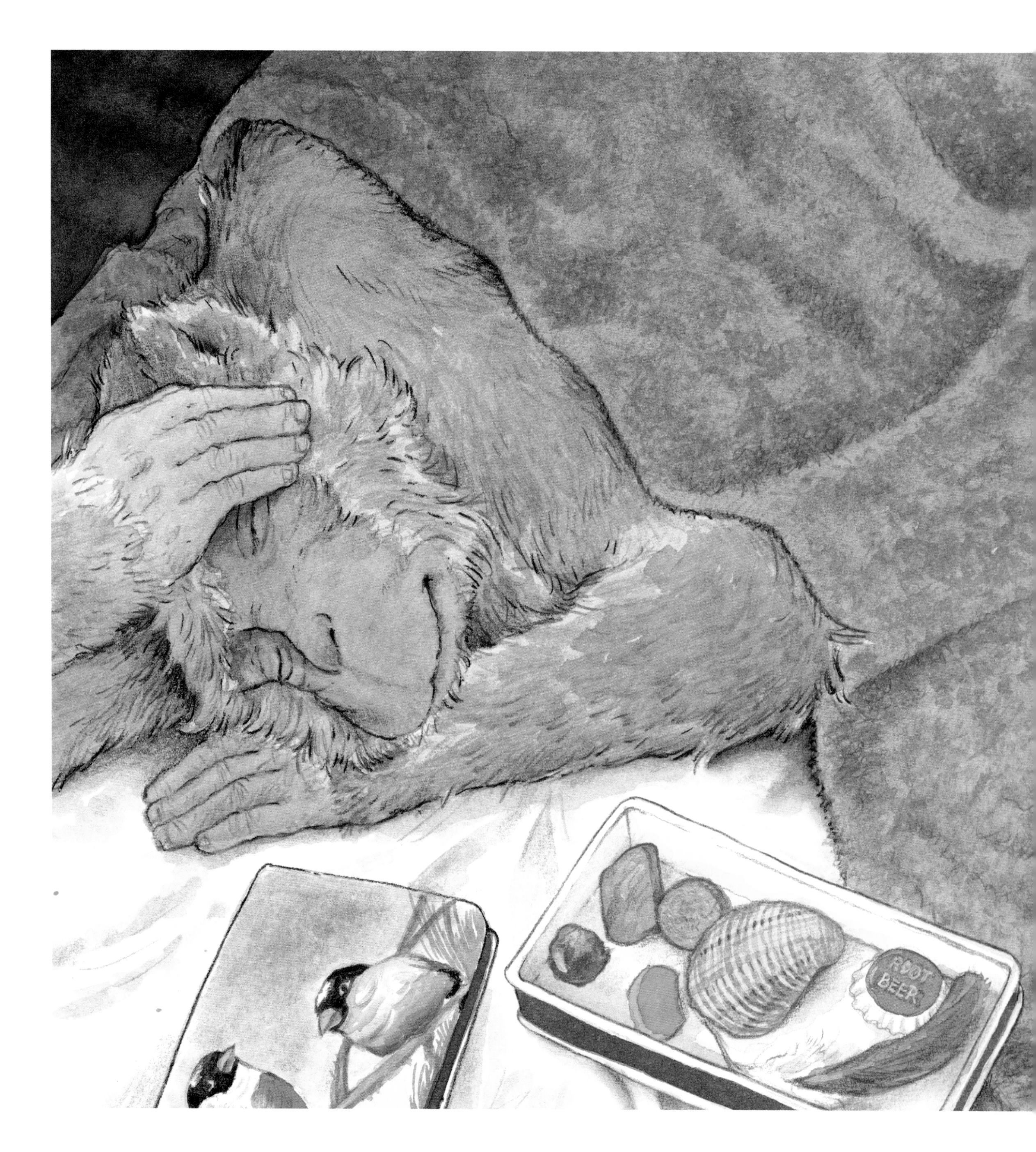

Woo kept her treasures in an old candy tin. Anything that caught her eye—small pebbles, feathers, and shells—went into the tin.

At night, Woo slept with her treasures close by.

No one wanted to buy Emily's art. To make a living, she made and sold clay bowls and hooked rugs. She raised and sold puppies.

Emily also rented rooms in her house on Simcoe Street.

The painter longed to paint. It was all Emily had ever wanted to do, but now she was too busy.

Emily bought a camper and called it the Elephant. It was tall and clumsy, but wonderful, just like an elephant. There was a place for everyone and everything.

Besides all her painting supplies, there was room for her dog Ginger Pop as well as Susie, Woo, and a cat or two.

Emily was planning another trip to the forest.

The night before her trip, Emily started packing. Woo helped by touching everything. Suddenly the little monkey took off.

She had found a new treasure.

Now I can pack in peace, thought Emily.
Later, packing would be the last thing on her mind.

Woo lay quietly on the floor. Her eyes were closed and she whimpered. Yellow paint covered her mouth and paws.

"Oh, Woo, what have you done?" sobbed Emily.
Woo had eaten her treasure, a tube of yellow paint.

The doctor came as quickly as he could. “This may help,” he said. He gave Woo medicine to help her throw up.

“We were going to the woods,” said Emily sadly. “Woo loves it there.”

“Paint is extremely dangerous,” said the doctor.
“I’m afraid that your monkey may not make it.”

Emily cradled Woo in her arms all night. She gently stroked the monkey and watched the beating of her tiny heart.

Emily prayed that somehow Woo would be strong enough to survive.

In the morning, the dawn's light woke Emily from a troubled sleep. Woo's eyes were open too!

The little monkey reached out her paw and softly murmured a tiny, "Woo." Emily took Woo's paw and smiled.

Cedars touched the sky. They touched the painter's heart too. For Woo, the forest was just like the jungle she remembered. Here, she felt free.

Woo and the painter breathed in the fragrance of earth and moss and tree. They felt the peace hidden in the heart of the rainforest.

Emily Carr was born in Victoria, British Columbia, in 1871—the same year the province became part of Canada. All her life, Emily was proud of the fact that she was the first in her family to be born a Canadian.

Emily began drawing when she was eight. Later, she studied painting in San Francisco, England, and France. But away from home, Emily always became ill; she was homesick for the wild beauty of Canada's West Coast.

When Emily returned home for good, she decided to paint the decaying totem poles on western Vancouver Island, Haida Gwaii, and the Skeena and Nass Rivers. She did not want these aspects of native culture to disappear into "silent nothingness." Emily gained the trust and respect of the First Nations people of Ucluelet, and they gave her the nickname "Klee Wyck," which means "Laughing One."

For many years, few people understood Emily's work. She couldn't sell her paintings and it was hard for her to make ends meet. So, in 1913, Emily built a house and rented rooms. She also bred and sold English sheepdogs and made and sold clay pottery. She did anything she could to make money. She even rented her own room, and lived in a tent in her backyard!

Then, in 1927, Emily was invited to exhibit her work in the National Gallery in Ottawa. This was the beginning of her most creative time. Soon Emily was making trips into the rainforest to paint its majestic beauty. When she could no longer paint, Emily began to write. Her first book, *Klee Wyck*, won the country's greatest literary honor, the Governor General's Award.

As she grew older, Emily Carr became ill and eventually could no longer care for her beloved pets. Before she died in 1945, Emily sent Woo to live in Vancouver's Stanley Park Zoo. Woo and Emily Carr had been the best of friends for fifteen years.